The JUDGE

STANLEY GRAHAM

authorHOUSE®

AuthorHouse™
1663 Liberty Drive
Bloomington, IN 47403
www.authorhouse.com
Phone: 1 (800) 839-8640

Published by AuthorHouse   01/29/2019

ISBN: 978-1-5462-7817-7 (sc)
ISBN: 978-1-5462-7816-0 (e)

Library of Congress Control Number: 2019901117

Print information available on the last page.

CONTENTS

CHAPTER 1

I HAVE DECIDED that this book can be classified as an autobiographical novel. Do not feel intimidated, and I am not putting it down. It is loosely based upon facts in my step-father's life, the subject of this novel. He is the main protagonist. My part is the secondary protagonist, the ;point of view of the teller of this story—"Rick.".

My stepfather (called Daddy by both my half-brother and myself) was born in Salem on the Lake, Ohio, in March 1877. Referred to as C.W. or Will or Willie, he had three brothers –Harry, Fred, and Walter –and two sisters—Frances ('Aunt Fannie') and Mamie who died in infancy.

Calvin William Appleby III, (usually called C.W. by his family) is the main protagonist. He had been married on December 30, 1902, to Elizabeth "Beth" Thompson, daughter of the local funeral director, ZH Thompson. Beth died October 24, 1920. This was their first marriage.

I need to use my imagination and visualize the life of the Applebys. Their ancestors included several captains of Steamships, including the Sultana, and ship builders and were some of the first settlers in Salem on the Lake in the early 1800s. In time, they had amassed a fortune and built a gigantic brick Victorian mansion on Main Street, near downtown. With three stories and a ballroom on the third, it was a prime example of ostentation and the largest house in town. Later, historians called it "the age of conspicuous consumption".

Many of the Appleby babies and small children died early or in infancy. The City Cemetery has a 50 ft. diameter circular lot dominated by a tall obelisk of red Vermont sandstone upon which are inscribed names and dates of birth and death. This obelisk is the tallest monument in the cemetery. It was transported by a railroad car from Vermont to Ohio and carved by an iterant sculptor, who lived upstairs in their carriage house during the winter he worked. (This account was told by "Aunt Fannie", the Judge's sister.)

A great deal of their money came from the sale of narrow (40 ft.) city lots. As the Judge "Daddy" recalled, "At one time my father owned almost all of Salem on the Lake—about two square miles. My father never worked. When he needed money, he sold lots." Another time, the Judge told about the sale of the land on both sides of Salem on the Lake harbor for the sum of $25,000, a veritable fortune in those days when working men earned only a dollar a day.

Their fortune enabled them to provide college educations for their children. They sent C.W. to Ohio State for his B.A. and to Cornell University where he graduated from the College of Law in 1898. Frances (Aunt Fannie) they sent to 2Oberlin College for her B.A. and to a teacher's college. She majored in history and political science. The younger brothers—Harry, Fred, and Walter they sent to Ohio University. Afterwards the sons married and helped their father in the family business of building and selling houses in the burgeoning city of Salem on the Lake.

The sons and their families moved into the largely vacant spacious family mansion; it had 12 bedrooms and 8 bathrooms, a formal small parlor, a larger family room, a library, a kitchen and pantry. Beth, especially after babies were born, was busy with overseeing the work of servants. At times it was almost too strenuous. At the end of a difficult day, she would take a hot bath and go to bed earlier than usual; she would turn her back on her husband when she suspected he wanted sex.

Eventually some of the Appleby investments failed and they had to pull in their horns, so to speak. However, the town's citizens regarded the Appleby families as rich and powerful. When asked by outsiders, they replied, "Oh, the Applebys, they're very rich."

C.W. (as the Judge was called in his youth and even by his first wife) lacked for nothing. His father and mother had kept him supplied with plenty of toys and candy. People said, "He's spoiled rotten. Whatever he wants, he gets." For dating, he had the use of his family's horse and buggy.

After C.W. graduated from college, his father gave him an all-expense-paid train trip through parts of Canada and the western states. He was accompanied by Tom Jones, his boyhood friend who was the same age and had wealthy and indulgent parents. The two young men had a wild time, especially in San Francisco where, in Chinatown, they visited an opium den. They saw eight or ten shirtless elderly Chinese men, reclining on low couches, connected by their hoses and pipes to a central apparatus in which opium was burning. They sucked on hoses and inhaled the smoke. The room was blue with the exhaled smoke which had a sickening sweet odor. One of the old smokers offered to let the boys suck on a hose. They said, "Thanks but no thanks." In later years C.W. told this story to anybody who would listen. It became part of his repertoire.

The Applebys were fond of parties and made good use of their third floor ballroom. Seemingly, they spared no expense and hired catering services and musicians. To be invited to one of their dinners and parties was a distinct honor. C.W. and his three brothers met and wooed their women in their third story ballroom. Above it was the fourth story tower, an interesting place for a son to bring his date when they wanted a little privacy. C.W.'s first wife Beth enjoyed these parties which she helped to plan. She was a small thin woman with jet black hair, always nicely combed. She was a good conversationalist; she could hold her own when discussing literary subjects. She was a graduate of the college of Wooster; she majored in English and history. She had various allergies which worsened during the dry days of August and September. She developed colds she could not shake. She died of pneumonia on October

24, 1920. She was buried with the deceased Applebys in the family plot dominated by the tall red Vermont sandstone obelisk.

Her husband C.W., her son Harrison and daughter Frances were devastated with grief. It was the ruination of their family. C.W. had two identical houses constructed on Liberty Street. They lived in one and rented out the other. C.W. had established a profitable law practice. He was a great talker and loved to argue, but he had nobody, it seemed, to share his grief. He was extremely handsome with dark wavy hair and a Charles Atlas physique. He was six foot four in his bare feet.

He walked to and from his office on Main Street. He tried to be jolly and sociable, but it was a strain. He needed help. He decided to join the Elks Club which was located on Main Street, just a block away. The fellows were drinking ale and beer. He drank a bottle and it seemed to help him forget his anxiety and his bitter memories. He recalled a line from a poem he read in college. It was *Terrence, This is stupid stuff* by A. E. Housman: "Gaze into the pewter pot and see the world as the world is not." The escape thrilled him, and he felt he had discovered a magic cure. One glass of beer led to another and to another and to another.

He began spending a lot of time at the Elks. One night he almost did not make it back to his house. Somehow he put one foot in front of another, holding on to black wrought iron fences, fell a few times and crawled the last fifty feet to his front porch steps. He was drunk, stinking drunk.

He was lucky this time. A neighbor Mr. Fred Griswold who rented the identical house next door, saw him stumbling and rushed to help him. He said, "Thanks….I know…..I've had too many…..but goddammit, I'm lonely….. and I don't care who knows it."

Mr. Fred Griswold, a friendly neighbor, helped him into the dark lonely house and up the stairs to the master bedroom. Mr. Griswold got him into bed, removed his shoes, and covered him with the extra blanket. The next morning he woke up with a headache and did not remember how he got home.

He knew he'd been drunk and his bad behavior would put him behind the eight ball. He had to get himself under control. *Thank God Harrison and Frances were not here.* A couple of months after Beth died, both children (now in their early twenties) left home. Harrison went to New York City, seeking work as a newspaper reporter. He had previously flunked out of two military academies and Frances was taking courses at Columbia University, preparing for a teaching career.

Eventually Frances met a young man from her hometown, Salem on the Lake, Bob Andrews, who was studying to become a landscape architect. Eventually he landed a well-paying job for the city of Washington D.C. He and Frances married. Frances became a working wife, teaching in a vocational high school. They had one daughter, Elizabeth who married Mike, a chemical engineer in Texas.

Harrison's career as a newspaper man fizzled, and he sought work elsewhere. He ended up as an elevator operator in one of the new skyscrapers in New York. The irony of his situation was that the cheap apartment he rented was on the fifth floor and he had to climb all those stairs after spending eight hours in an elevator. After eating a frugal supper with his wife and four children, two boys and two girls, he was so exhausted that he was almost too tired to help or enjoy his family. He had some mental issues of his own, having flunked out of two military academies, incurring the wrath of his lawyer father. His conscience bothered him because he could not provide a better life for his family. Troubled by financial worries, he tried desperately to make ends meet. He accepted begrudgingly generous checks from his father. Every time he cashed one at the bank, he cringed. Memories of the ornate mansion of his grandparents and parties in the third floor ballroom haunted him nearly all the time.

C.W.'s lawyer's office was on the second floor of one of the buildings in downtown Salem on the Lake. There was only one building taller and it was the three story Pelton's Department Store.

It was owned by Arvine Pelton, an eccentric who owned and supervised daily operations from his second floor balcony. Many stories were told of his eccentricity and his penurious habits. "I'll bet he's framed the first dollar he ever earned," C.W. often quoted

C.W.'s lawyer's office was upstairs in one of the two story buildings. It was located in the central part of the building with no windows. Instead, it had a large sky-lite. Furniture consisted of a mammoth roll-top desk with numerous cubbyholes into which papers could be filed, four uncomfortable black horse hair upholstered chairs, a long black leather couch with a headrest where C.W. took his naps, bookcases filled with fat law books, and two green wooden filing cabinets. The only picture on the four walls was a lithograph of the steamship Sultana, one of the early side-wheelers, captained by his grandfather—Calvin W. Appleby (1808 – 1880)

C.W. was proud of his illustrious ancestry and told stories which had been in newspapers. The Salem News Herald (Feb. 18, 1950) published the following: "Throughout the Great Lakes region he had a reputation as a builder and skipper of some of the finest ships on the Great Lakes.

"And the finest of them all was the passenger side-wheeler Sultana of which he was captain for a number of years.

"The Sultana known as the 'floating palace' of the Great Lakes was the last word in luxury in the lake travel of the day. A fountain played on its deck, and hand painted oil pictures adorned the stateroom doors. Cabins contained comforts for passengers unheard of on most other ships of the day."

C.W.'s law practice was fairly profitable. Stories like the one just quoted helped to attract clients. Beth, his wife, said that his office, at the end of a long flight of dirty and dark stairs, was ugly; it needed a woman's touch, but C.W. usually replied, "Bosh. It's OK the way it is. I know exactly where everything is."

Despite his assertion otherwise, he often spent much time searching for valuable papers. Beth wanted him to move into a first floor office, but he never did.

After her death, during the next ten years, he regretted that he had not paid much attention to her ideas about a better office. The fact is, he did not want to have a better office. He would joke and say, "A woman's place is in the home. And that is where she belongs when she gets off work." Beth said, "That's a cruel joke C.W." Putting women down was one of C.W.'s worse traits.

Another joke was:

Joe says, "I got a dog for my wife." Moe says, "Hey, Good trade!" Ha, Ha, Ha.

"That's just horrible," said his wife.

"Well, I'm sorry I told it. I'm just trying to put a little humor into our lives."

"But not at my expense." Beth crossed her arms. She had stood her ground. She said, "C.W., what I am mostly concerned about is our continuing to live in this old mansion. We told your three brothers and families they could move in, but I think that was a mistake. Who's in charge? You're too busy with your job as the Judge to know what is going on here. This drafty old place with the twelve foot ceilings is just too much for me. It's a hullabaloo of noise most of the time when the kids are home from school or college. I try to be in charge and set forth a few simple rules, but they are never obeyed. I'm just sick and tired of being sick and tired." She had been standing at the sink in the huge kitchen.

"You'd better sit down," said her husband. The Judge recalled this bitter memory before Beth died and before he had decided to build two new houses on Liberty Street. He had moved Beth into one of the newly finished houses. The day they moved in Beth began cleaning all the windows. The poor woman did not have time to enjoy the house before she died.

The days after the funeral were the saddest ones in his entire life. He never knew how devastating it would be. Often he could hardly control his crying. His three brothers tried to console him and invited him for family dinners. The three wives did the same and sent him home with left overs. All he had to do was warm them up in the oven.

On her death bed Beth had said to C.W: "I want you to get married again. You are still a young man." C.W. wept openly; he could not control himself. Beth had been such a good woman. He wondered if he'd ever find another one like her.

Harrison and Frances had come for the funeral. Frances had brought her young husband Bob Andrews. Harrison came alone, leaving his family of four children and his wife in the fifth floor apartment in New York City.

CHAPTER 2

THUS, TIME PASSED and C.W. began thinking about finding the right woman and remarrying. He was now in his late fifties and he had recently been elected as the first Municipal Court Judge He was tired of making the various stump speeches, but he was glad to be elected. Just walking down the street caused passers-by to wave and greet him joyfully. It felt good. It was the year 1928, the year in which his stepson Richard "Rick" Stevens was born. [C.W., of course, knew nothing about Richard Stevens "Rick" before his second marriage.]

C.W. had long since moved out of the family mansion and into one of the two identical houses on Liberty Street. His three brothers and families remained in the family mansion.

The reason C.W. moved out was that he began seeing images of his deceased wife almost everywhere, especially at night when he was undressing and putting on his pajamas. His wife would be floating, wearing nothing but a flimsy transparent nightgown, toward him. She whispered, "I want you to make love to me, C.W." He extended his hand, and it passed through the image.

The first time this happened he nearly went out of his mind. Rationally, he told himself, "This is a hallucination." It was hard to predict when or where the next visit would occur. He told himself that his dead wife was a ghost haunting the mansion. He did not dare tell this to anyone; they would think he was crazy, that he had lost his marbles, that he had bats in his belfry, that he was nuts.

One night he climbed the stairs to the third floor ballroom and saw her dancing by herself, wearing the same transparent nightgown. She thrust her arms forward, seemingly to invite him to dance with her. C.W. took two steps forward, and the image disappeared. For a long time, he lay awake in his lonely bed.

Throughout his career as a lawyer and attorney at law, C.W. nearly always managed to keep his work life and his family life separate. The years after Beth died in October, 1920, and until 1930 when he remarried were busy ones. C.W. was determined to become an excellent lawyer who won nearly all of his cases. An interesting case involving a jury trial was that of Frank Feathers. C.W.'s defense was persuasive and the visiting judge's instructions to the jury members were explicit and detailed, running to eight typewritten pages. "The defendant, Frank Feathers, is on trial upon an affidavit filed in this case against him, charged with the offense of assault and battery in the city of Salem on the Lake, Indianola County, Ohio. The charges that the said Frank Feathers, on or about the first day of September, 1925, unlawfully assaulted and struck Albert Pape, contrary to the provisions of the Revised Code of Ohio."

"Frank Feathers has pleaded not guilty and denied each and every allegation made against him in the affidavit. There was much more legal language. C.W. had been assigned to defend Frank Feathers, and he delivered what the jury members called "a magnificent and heartrending defense." C.W. was pleased and proud of himself when he heard the verdict NOT GUILTY. He overheard some of the comments of the police who had testified. In a stage whisper, they were saying "bum verdict."

This happened quite often. C.W. tried to ignore it and move on.

When he was not busy with court work, C.W. often thought about his late wife Beth. He recalled her saying. "C.W. darling, you should marry again." The death-bed scene played in his head, and he helped it go away by reading biographies and novels. He was extremely intelligent.

His score on his bar examination was the second highest in the state of Ohio. In college he was a member of the honorary fraternity Phi Beta Kappa. He kept the Phi Beta key in his vest pocket; it was attached to a chain he whirled when he was bored. His wife Beth was patient with him and tried to understand his occasional tirades and his assertions of his superiority. He felt he was better and wiser than any man or woman in the town, if not in the entire world. Beth called it "a superiority complex." He told her, "My father told me that I was the smartest boy and man in this town." He bragged about his grandfathers who had captained passenger ships on the Great Lakes and transported negro runaway slaves to Canada. The grandfathers were considered agents in the Underground Railroad. They had to be secretive and not let anyone know what they were doing. It was a federal crime to aid the runaway slaves and they could be jailed and/or fined.

He especially enjoyed historical novels and later murder mysteries.

He renewed his membership in the Elks club and began making evening visits to drink beer and socialize. He was popular and well-liked by the majority of men in the town. As for the women, he was not certain; he had not found any woman with whom he wanted to spend the rest of his life.

He let it be known among the drinking crowds that he was searching for a wife. The year was now 1930

He remembered Willie Bradley and some of his drinking bouts at the Blue Moon, the roadhouse of Willie and his wife Florence. He visited their roadhouse once more. He saw Willie busy behind the bar and told him about his wanting to meet women.

"Do you want a one night stand?"

"Hell, no, I want a beautiful vivacious good woman with whom I can fall in love. If I find her, I want to marry her."

"So you're really serious about this marriage bit?"

"Yes. I thought I could do everything by myself, but I get lonely. When I leave the court houses each day, it would be nice to go home to a good woman who has cooked a nourishing meal."

"Okay, Judge I'll see what I can do. I have a cousin Ada who is a divorcee with two children. Right now she and the children are living with her parents in the family farmhouse. Its south of Geneva at a little crossroads called Harpers Field. When I get off work, I'll call her."

The Judge was not sure about whether Willie would check into it, but he'd give Willie the benefit of the doubt.

He was surprised the next day when Willie telephoned and said he'd make arrangements for the Judge to meet Ada at their roadhouse called The Blue Moon, five miles west of Salem on the Lake.

Ada persuaded her brother Guy, five years her senior, to drive her to the Blue Moon to meet the Judge. Guy was living and working at the family Farm and had been for several years. Ada thought that Guy resembled Humphrey Bogart she'd seen in some of his movies. Usually Guy went about his work unshaven and shirtless most of the time.

He said to his sister, "I think you might be better off getting married to Frank Feather. He says he probably could fall in love with you. He'll inherit his parents' farm since he's the only offspring...."

Ada said, "Guy, I've got as mind of my own. It's my life and I want to make the best choice for a husband."

"What do you and the Judge have in common? I've read about him in the newspapers. He comes from a wealthy family and a lot of them live in that Victorian mansion in Salem on the Lake. The article in the papers said they can trace their ancestors and settlers back to the early 1800s when land was cheap as dirt—25 cents per acre."

"I don't care about his ancestors buried in the City Cemetery. Papa said to me, 'As long as you're getting married is concerned, you might as well marry a rich man.' I'd like to meet him and make up my own mind."

Guy said, "Let's make it a double date. I've been seeing a nice woman—Nancy Jones. I'll ask her. She's a grade school teacher in a country school. She will sit next to me in the front seat and you and the Judge will ride in the rumble seat. [The car was a black Model T Ford.] I'll have a blanket to keep you and the Judge warm and cozy. We'll have a great time."

Forty minutes later they were in the parking lot of the Blue Moon. The parking lot was really what was left of the front yard grass, mostly missing. The U-shaped driveway was shaded by ancient Sycamore trees the bark of which was peeling off in long messy strips. Molly said, "I'm glad this is out of town. If anybody sees me going into a place where beer and liquor are served, I'd lose my job." [These were the Prohibition days in the early 1930s.]

Guy said, "Molly, don't worry about that. In case you are spotted, I'll say you are my cousin and I planned a little Birthday party for you."

The house, remodeled to make a tavern, was a bungalow-style structure, painted white with a wide front porch, located about 500 ft. from the road, busy Rt. 20. There was, of course, no large painted sign indicating that this was the Bradley Roadhouse. Strangers driving on the highway would perhaps have noted the presence of many cars parked in the front yard and concluded this was a family gathering or reunion, but knowledgeable Salem on the Lake people knew better and were not fooled.

Ada was nervous as she climbed out of the front seat and walked with Guy and Molly toward the front screen door. She heard the music from the nickelodeon and recognized the tune: *Has Anybody seen my gal?* She wondered, *What am I getting into?*

Upon entering and after adjusting to the dim lighting, Ada observed the men seemed to outnumber the women three to one. Most of the women present appeared to be on the dance floor with their men partners. It was warm and stuffy inside and alcoholic fumes permeated the air. The windows were wide open and electric fans kept the air stirring.

Ada soon found Florence, wrapped in a white apron around her massive middle, carrying a tray of bottles and glasses to a table of six young men, all dressed in jeans and plaid cotton shirts. Florence smiled, flirted, and made small talk with them as she unloaded the bottles and glasses.

When she left this table, a man at another table yelled at her, "Hey, where's our beers?"

She smiled at him and said, "Hold your horses, honey, be right with you."

She had briefly seen Ada, Guy, and Molly who were now waiting next to the bar chatting with Willie, her husband, who was acting as bartender. She rushed over to them. "Glad you could make it. Follow me. The Judge is waiting at a table in that far corner." She led them there.

The same man yelled angrily, "Hey, where's our beers?"

As she passed him, she patted his leg flirtatiously and said again, "Hold your horses, honey. I'll be back in a minute." The man calmed down.

The Judge stood up as they approached. Florence said to him, "Judge Appleby, "I'd like you to meet my cousin, Ada Bradley." He took Ada's hand in his. Then Florence introduced Guy and Molly.

As they sat down, Judge Appleby said to them, "What would you like to drink? Gin and tonics? That's what I'm drinking. It's on me."

Ada thought he had a beautiful harmonious voice well modulated--the kind of voice which, if its volume were increased, could be easily heard everywhere in a courtroom.

Ada was flustered, she had never had a gin and tonic. Since she did not want to experiment, she said, "Just a glass of wine. Guy and Molly ordered the same.

Guy and Molly stood up and joined the dancers and Ada and the Judge were alone. The Judge was immaculately attired, considering it was a hot summer day, in an ivory colored Palm Beach suit, a white shirt with a pink tie and cuff links. Ada felt she was under-dressed in her simple pink cotton outfit with lace trim and white beads. She had not worn her suit jacket because it was so warm. Now she kind of wished she had.

As they made small talk, Ada tried to guess the Judge's age. His hair was light brown and his face was unlined. He had a slightly aquiline nose, light blue eyes, and a trim physique. He was, she thought, rather handsome and distinguished looking. She guessed he must be in his early to mid-forties.

He made polite inquiries about her present living arrangements with her parents at Harpers Field. She told him she was divorced with two children, but she did not describe Janet's condition. If he knew how bad Janet's condition really was, he would probably drop her like a hot potato.

She was pleased that he was interested in getting to know her. He seemed impressed by her easy-going manner and stunning beauty. He smiled broadly and told her, "You know, you are a very beautiful woman."

Ada blushed. Other men had told her the same and she regarded it as a pick-up line. Nevertheless, it made her feel good.

There was a lull in their conversation and Ada did not know what to say. To break the ice, the Judge said, "Why don't you call me Will? And everybody calls you Ada ?"

My sisters call me and my twin sister Babe."

"Babe, that's strange. How did they come up with Babe?"

"When my twin sister and I were about five or six years old, we were lost in the woods for a couple of hours. You know, Babes in the Woods."

The Judge smiled. "That's cute. Why don't we dance Babe?" he said, standing up and taking her hand. "I'd like to get to know <u>this</u> Babe," he added, putting strong emphasis upon the word <u>this.</u>

He was a skillful dancer, and she liked the considerate way he held her—no mushy intimacy, no vulgar contact on a first date. Ada was also impressed by the good humored remarks, the friendly greetings, and the awe with which he was regarded by almost everyone in the large room. Florence said he was popular with Salem on the Lake people, and she saw evidence of it the very first time she met him. The nickelodeon was playing a recent hit "Come and Dance With Me" The constant repetition of the same words and the background music and blue smoke lent a charming ambience to the room. It was the year the word ambience was becoming popular. Back at their table he asked her if he could call on her. He asked "How about tomorrow afternoon? Do you have anything planned? How about 2:00 p.m.?" And, so it was arranged that he would drive to the Farm. Guy gave him directions.

Sunday proved to be another beautiful day with a clear blue sky and white fluffy cumulus clouds. When he arrived, Ada introduced him to her parents and her two-year-old blonde haired, blue-eyed toddler, Rick. The Judge was attired in the same type of suit he wore at Bradley's Roadhouse. Ada knew that her parents were very much impressed by his courtly and gentlemanly ways. He sat down on a chair in the Farm's sitting room.

The Judge looked around the sitting room. Its chairs and an antique settee could seat about ten or twelve people.

The Judge said, "How about your daughter? Do I get to meet her?"

"Oh, …she's asleep upstairs. She always takes a nap at this time." Ada hoped her voice was steady. Now was definitely not the time to show off the little girl. Ada did not want to strike out before she had a chance to know this new man.

When Ada saw the Judge's shiny yellow automobile with its black top, black fenders, and black running boards she was flabbergasted. "It's beautiful," she exclaimed.

"I just bought it a couple of weeks ago. The salesman called it a '1930 Model A Ford Victoria. Does that long name impress you?" He laughed, showing his even white teeth.

Ada was tremendously impressed. *This man must have money. He must be loaded with deep pockets, and he's interested in me. It's almost like a dream come true. What* little Ada knew about wealthy people was largely derived from the movies Harry Feather had taken her to. She felt somewhat guilty about going out with the Judge while her relationship with Harry was still in limbo. But she felt she had to look out for herself and her children. She asked herself, What is the best deal for me?

First, he drove down to the Grand River, through the covered bridge, and parked on the south side of the river. There were a few picnic tables about, and he chose one close to the river.

"This is called a river, but it's more like a creek or crick as we used to call it.

"It looks as though you could wade across it," she said.

"I'm sure you could," he remarked. "Movies always show people slipping on the rocks and falling into the water. I shall not do that!" He smiled, showing his white even teeth again. He had a nice smile, appropriate to use when he agreed with the verdict in an important case. In his mind-set, whatever that all entailed, he never really got away from a well-organized and well attended court room. Anyhow, this date with Ada, he mused, would be an attempt to do so. He needed a change of scenery, and he enjoyed seeing a beautiful new face—that of Ada Bradley Stevens. Where had she been all during his previous life? He felt he was on the verge of falling in love, and he began asking questions as all lovers do.

Ada was thinking that this was a lame beginning, but it's better than nothing. She almost dozed but caught herself. She heard the Judge saying, "Usually when a fellow dates a lady for the first time, he takes her to dinner or a picture show, but I figured we could talk right here. It's warm enough. Then I'll take you for a drive along the lake, and then I'll take you to dinner. How does that sound?"

"Great," Ada exclaimed and smiled sweetly. She was overwhelmed.

"Well, who goes first?" he asked.

"What do you mean?"

"Do I tell my story first? Or do you?"

"Well, why don't you tell me about yourself? My cousin Willie Bradley said your ancestors were some of the first settlers in Salem on the Lake…"

"That's a good beginning. I'll tell you what has been told to me many times. In the 1820s my grandfather, who by the way has the same name as mine—Calvin William Appleby—came with his family from Bethlehem, New Hampshire, to the Salem on the Lake area, first explored by Moses Cleveland in1798. This land became known as part of the Western Reserve of Connecticut. It extended from there to the Mississippi River, available for purchase by pioneers at the amazingly low price of 25 cents per acre or even lower in some places. Anyhow, my grandfather bought about 700 acres, more than a square mile. At first, he farmed some of it Sometime later he became, in the prime of his life, one of the steamboat captains of the Great Lakes, the skipper of one of the finest ships on the Lakes—the passenger side-wheeler –the Sultana. By the way, I am the proud owner of a framed lithograph of this ship. I'll show it to you sometime later."

"Anyhow, this ship became known as the floating palace of the Great Lakes. It was the last word in luxury lake travel of the day. A fountain played on its deck and oil paintings adorned the stateroom doors, many of them hand painted by a little known artist, Randolph 'Randy'Brown a native of Salem on the Lake. It was a real luxury liner.

"Calvin W. Appleby, the skipper of the Sultana, encouraged his younger brother, Galvin, to work his way up from deckhand to the skipper of a sister ship—the Ohioanna.

"Below decks on both ships, all kinds of packaged freight was carried. Before and during the Civil War the cargoes included runaway slaves who hid among the boxes and barrels of the Applebys' ships. The two Appleby skippers helped the slaves on the last leg of their flights to freedom in Canada and deposited them in Canadian territory at the mouth of the Detroit river.

"Both brothers were dedicated abolitionists and took in slaves that had been whisked the length of Ohio from slavery to freedom by zealous Underground Railroad workers. You know, at that time, Ohio and this section of the state was a strong antislavery area. Some of Salem on the Lakes leading citizens hid slaves in their attics and cellars, giving them shelter and food. For example, Dr. Leet's house in Salem on the Lake had a trapdoor in the kitchen, hidden beneath a hooked rug. The trapdoor led to a cellar where they hid slaves."

[Dr. Leet's house, still maintained by its present owners, is close to the downtown and the Appleby four-story mansion. Both houses are listed in the National Register of Historic Places.]

"I forgot to mention that both ships, usually running from Buffalo to Chicago, Cleveland, and many ports between, had casinos and gambling was permitted and encouraged. The two owners and brothers, profited from gambling. Their motto was: 'The House always wins.'. The fortune they earned helped to construct the Appleby Mansion in Salem on the Lake. Its cost was about five hundred thousand dollars. In today's dollars, it would be many times more—in the millions."

The Judge stopped to catch his breath. I hope I'm not boring you with all this history, but I am very proud of my two skippers of the Sultana and the Ohioanna. In addition to making a fortune, they freed thousands of slaves."

"Oh, no. I am fascinated. I always liked studying history in school, but you make it come alive. By the way do you have any personal memories of your grandfather and great uncle?"

"Not really. My grandfather died when I was three years old. My great uncle died a few years later. I have fuzzy memories of a man with a white beard...."

Ada quickly thought she'd inject some humor into this long monologue. "You're sure it wasn't Santa Claus." She smiled sweetly.

The Judge liked her comment and laughed. "No. Everything I've told you was told to me. Family stories. Also, I've done a lot of reading."

The Judge had been careful to tell her only the good things; there were many skeletons in his and his families' closets, but he did not want to unlock all those doors yet. He said to Ada, "Why don't you tell me about some of your adventures?"

"Not nearly as impressive as yours," she said, but she told about the business college that she and her sister Eva had attended after graduating from Peru High School, in Indiana. She told about their exciting jobs in the State, War and Navy Building "right next to the White House." they were able to obtain passes for short visits.

She did explain how she met her first husband—a Major in the Marine Corps—at a YWCA dance. She glossed over their marital problems and eventual divorce. *Too much dirty linen* she phrased in her mind.

By the time he drove her back to the Farm, it was bout 7:p.m. He accompanied her to the front door and told her, "I had a wonderful time with you, Ada. Could we do something like this next Sunday. Maybe take in a movie too."

Ada was somewhat surprised by his interest. She had pictured herself as sort of a plain Jane in the academic and intellectual departments. Apparently the Judge appreciated her beauty; he had told her, as other men had, that she was beautiful. Ada usually considered it as a pick-up line.

But Florence had told her the same thing. It was ego-inflating to hear these compliments. Later in the evening she told some of the Judge's stories to her parents. They were greatly impressed.

Her father laughed and said again, "If you are going to fall in love and marry, you might as well fall in love and marry a rich man."

Her brother Guy was not as impressed as his parents "I have the gut feeling that he's a big phony. Sounds like a pompous windbag—like all the politicians. He knows how to talk"

"Guy," she interrupted him. "He's really a very nice man. How can you say such things?"

Guy said, "How about Harry Feather, the chicken farmer" Guy wanted her to marry his good friend, the chicken farmer. Harry had dreams of becoming a great success like that guy in the next state south –Kentucky. He'd advertise: OHIO FRIED CHICKEN. The advent of frozen poultry and meats was a boon to fast food businesses.

Guy had to laugh. He had once told Harry to look for some kind of business that did not involve chickens. This was before freezers became abundant and popular. Now Harry and Guy liked the slogans of the younger generation: FAST FOOD, FAST CARS, and FAST WOMEN.

CHAPTER 3

JUDGE APPLEBY KNEW he had struck gold when he met and began courting Ada Stevens. He dated her on several Sunday afternoons that summer of 1930. She was a charming and beautiful woman in her early thirties. The fact that she had not gone to college did not bother him in the least. She would make a good life and home for him. It had been ten years since his first wife Beth Thompson died, and he was a lonely man; His two grown children –Harrison and Frances—were married and living in Washington D.C/.and New York City.—He seldom saw them.

The Judge did not especially like having a ready-made family – a 2 ½ year old stepson Rick Sevens who seemed normal and his sister Janet, 8 years old, who was anything but normal. If she could not learn, he would see to it that she was placed in an institution for the feeble minded; this was located in Columbus. The Judge had driven by its heavy wrought iron gates several times, and the entire three story building constructed of Ohio's Berea brown sandstone looked foreboding to him. He hoped he'd never see the inside of the place and its unfortunate inmates. Little did he know that someday he would be taking Janet there.

The Judge was careful about his musings; they often occurred while he was driving, and he recited them aloud. He was worried about the possibility of his falling asleep while driving. He had more than enough cases of this nature confronting him day by day.

On a Saturday evening while he was driving back from a date with Ada, he decided he would ask her to marry him. He figured he'd stop at Bradley's roadhouse, talk with Willie and Florence Bradley, and have a couple of gin and tonics before returning to his house on Liberty Street. He said to himself, *"I showed this Victorian house to Ada once and I could tell that she hated it. I've got a big brick bungalow in mind that I think she'll like."*

Anyhow, he resolved not to think too much about their future habitat.

He mused about the very existence of places like Bradley's Roadhouse all over the country. In the cities they were called "speakeasies." Bradley's, as the drinking crowd was well aware, was not a high class establishment, merely a place to have a few drinks and socialize and make new friends.

The fact that it existed at all and had not been closed down by the police indicated that Prohibition was not uniformly enforced; in fact, it was flagrantly violated everywhere.

The Judge predicted that the 18th Amendment to the U.S. Constitution that prohibited all alcoholic beverages in the United States would be repealed. He, himself, had been drinking his entire life, before and all during Prohibition, and he saw nothing wrong with it. He did not believe in obeying laws with which he strongly disagreed.

He often compared Prohibition with the Fugitive Slave Laws prior to the Civil War. If everyone had obeyed those laws, no runaway slaves would have ever reached Canada. There would have been no Underground Railroad. Novels such as Uncle Tom's Cabin and Huckleberry Finn would never have been written; Huck Finn would never have helped Jim, a runaway slave, to escape from the bounty hunters.

Once, a young woman in her early 20s confronted the Judge on the sidewalk in front of the City Courthouse by stopping in front of him and saying "Isn't it your duty to enforce these laws?"

The Judge was momentarily distracted and could not recall where he had seen her before this meeting. Never mind, it will come to me, he thought.

In the meantime he answered her question in his usual way. He said, "Yes, I am required to enforce laws. However, if I feel that the laws are fundamentally unfair, I believe it is my civic duty to disobey them. I believe it is my civic duty to disobey unfair laws. I fear I am repeating myself." The Judge looked around and saw that a small gathering of citizens were hanging onto every word. One of them, a well-dressed man in his mid-thirties, holding a small notebook, spoke up, "Judge, I have supported you most of the time, but I can't with this matter." He left and the small crowd broke up.

The Judge went to bed early that night, but his sleep was interrupted with horrible dreams. He dreamed he was delivering speeches on street corners. Oh, yes, he knew about the evils of alcohol. But he also preached "all things in moderation." He did not always practice what he preached. He recalled times when he had been stinking drunk, especially after his first wife died in 1920. He knew exactly why he got drunk. It was to dull the pain caused by Beth's death and the ensuing loneliness. He missed her company during the day and their sexual life at night. Nights were hard to endure without the help of alcohol.

At first the Judge drank only beer. Lately he had been trying gin and tonics. He was cognizant of the fact that alcohol loosened his tongue; he was much more talkative after consuming a few drinks, and he struck up conversations with citizens at Bradley's and other bars in Salem on the Lake. He was a dyed-in-the-wool Republican and expounded the views of that party. Outwardly, he was friendly and convivial with everyone.

For that reason and his good reputation as a lawyer, he was well-liked and popular with the majority of people in Salem on the Lake. Most of them forgave his drinking and drunken spells; after all, he drank only on weekends and was completely sober on weekdays. His drinking did not affect his work as a Judge. They elected him as their Municipal Court Judge in 1930 and continued voting for him until 1957. He served as Judge until a few days before his death in September, 1957—nearly 27 years.

CHAPTER 4

AFTER THE JUDGE arrived at Bradley's he told Florence and Willie I'm sure glad you introduced me to Ada. "I know she'll make an ideal wife. I'm going to ask her to marry me."

Florence smiled broadly. She was pleased to know she had been successful in playing cupid. "So you haven't asked her yet?"

"We've talked about marriage. But I have made up my mind. I'm going to ask her next Saturday. Don't tell her in the meantime. They don't have a telephone anyhow. You're the only people I've told. I'm really happy."

Willie extended his hand to the Judge. "Congratulations! When will it be?"

"The sooner the better, we'll probably have a low-key ceremony and just have a Justice of the Peace I know in Jefferson marry us."

As the Judge drove to his house on Liberty Street, he thought about how his career would be enhanced by the presence of a charming and beautiful wife.

He believed she was in her early thirties—34 as Florence had told him—but he had not told Ada his exact age of 54—20 years older. Friends had told him he appeared to be in his early forties, so he'd leave Ada with that impression. He did not want her to feel she was marrying an old man. That might convince her not to marry him. In fact, he decided that if she asked him, "How old are you?" he would lie and say

25

44. Ten years her senior sounded better than 20 years her senior. He did not want to spoil his chances for marriage.

In the meantime, Harry Feather had not been happy with Ada's dating Judge Appleby. Ada told him the Judge was interested. Harry tried harder to persuade Ada to marry him (Harry). During their few dates he intensified his kissing. Ada, sensing his desperate need and love for her, was emotionally and sexually attracted. Harry was indeed, a handsome and well- endowed muscular man, whereas Judge Appleby, though trim and a natty dresser, was flabby in comparison.

Ada's brother, Guy Bradley, extolled Harry's virtues and decried C.W.'s pomposity. "Harry really loves you, Ada. Has the Judge ever told you he loves you?"

"Not yet, but I think he will...soon. I have the feeling he'll ask me to marry him...maybe even next Saturday."

Ada's parents were of the opinion that the Judge would make the better husband. Her father said, "You've got to think about your future and the future of your children. Judge Appleby has an excellent position and will be a good provider. He has much more money, and he can earn more money than Harry will. You can't rely on farming—especially chicken farming—for security. Egg prices fluctuate wildly. When the price goes down, you can lose your shirt. If you marry Harry, you may be poverty-stricken the rest of your life."

He made a strong case for Ada not to marry the Judge, and her mother agreed it was the wise thing to do. She protested somewhat feebly. "I'm not sure I love him or if I can love him. We've never really kissed very much." She was thinking about Harry's ardor. "I know Harry loves me, and I think I can love him in return. He's hell-bent on marrying me."

Her brother Guy said, "Follow you heart. Don't just marry for money or security. Marry for Love. If Harry really loves you, you can't go wrong with him."

The following Saturday, during a candlelight dinner at a swanky restaurant in Indianola, Judge Appleby formally professed his love and proposed. "Ada, I know I am in love with you. I hope that, in time, you can love me." He reached for her left hand and said, "Will you marry me?"

Ada had been expecting this, but it was still something of a surprise. She thought about Harry. She was almost speechless and hesitated. She looked into his pale blue eyes as he held her hand and said, "To be honest, I've got to think seriously about it.'

"What's there to think about? I can offer you love, security and new home for us and your two children. And I think we should have one or more children of our own."

"Will," she said She still felt somewhat uneasy about using his first name. She always thought of him as the Judge—not as Will or Willie or CW. This time, she called him "Will."

She repeated his name, getting used to it, "There's something I have not told you yet...I didn't want to tell you...But I have had another offer of marriage...."

The Judge's face turned crimson and the corners of his mouth turned downward. "No, I never suspected. I hope I am the better man." After that, conversation was difficult, and Ada was relieved when their date ended. After he escorted her to the front door, he kissed her chastely on her right cheek, as he always did.

did.

"I really did have a good time tonight Will, and I'm pleased you asked me to marry you. I'll think seriously about it."

Harry said, "I know I've said all this before and I'll say I all again. DITTO."

He turned around and walked slowly, head downward, to his chrome yellow Ford Victoria automobile.

Ada awoke late one morning in mid-October, looked out the window, and saw it was another beautiful day. It was one of those gorgeous blue and gold October days. The sky was a pale blue with a few white cumulus clouds. The leaves of the locust and birch trees were a brilliant gold and the oak trees a reddish brown.

The lovely day should have uplifted Ada's spirits. She was in the doldrums. After washing and dressing Rick and Janet, she led them downstairs to the kitchen. Her mother was standing in her usual place, before the mammoth black iron stove, cooking oatmeal.

"How'd you sleep, Ada ? Her mother inquired.

"Not too well, too many dreams. One I remember is walking along a gravel road in a big forest, giant trees everywhere. Then I come to a fork in the road, and I don't know what to do. I'm panic stricken. I can't move. And then I wake up. Several times last night I had the same dream."

Her mother set bowls of steaming oatmeal on the table. She said, "I think you know what that means Ada."

"Yes…Who should I marry, Harry Feather or Judge Appleby?"

Her father opened the back door, entered, went into the pantry, and used the lift pump to bring up some cold water from the cistern. He washed his hands with the yellow bar of P&G soap; it never made a good suds, as Rick recalled. Her father sat down in his Captain's chair. It that was well-worn and somewhat wobbly at the head of the table. He took his time and looked at each person. He said to his daughter, Ada, "Why so glum, Ada?

"Same old thing Papa, what should I do? Who—or whom-- should I marry?"

"My dear girl, you know what we advised you to do –JUDGE APPLEBY."

"But I think I am really in love with Harry. I almost told him that." Lately he had been very attentive and had proclaimed his love repeatedly. He showed her his plans for building a house several hundred feet away from his parents' farm-house. He had already contacted a contactor friend and also a loan officer at the bank. Both houses would be atop a long glacial ridge which separated them from a rocky pasture. Harry was very enthusiastic about this project and said many times, "We'll be able to sit on our front porch and have wonderful views of both sunrise and sunset. Ada, I can just picture this house of our own. Come with me and be my life's partner." He had been jumping about while explaining the layout. He could hardly sit still. They were sitting on folding lawn chairs in the backyard of his parents' farmhouse. The weather had become colder and Harry had brought sweaters and blankets.

CHAPTER 5

DURING A FEW days few days in late October, 1930, the temperature was unusually warm and balmy and climbing into the 80's in the afternoons. Harry began thinking of a new way to persuade Ada to marry him. Maybe the scientists were correct in their claims that there was a world-wide climate change taking place—hotter winters and colder summers, continental glaciers melting.

Anyhow, the sudden very warm days in late October would help me, he thought to himself in his matrimonial pursuit. Thus far, Harry had wined and dined Ada. He had taken her to movies and to a few dinners in ritzy restaurants and had kissed her in the front seat of his black Ford pick-up truck parked next to the barn, but he figured he had never properly wooed her.

Because the weather was so warm, the ideal setting for this adventure might be his old rocky beach and swimming hole in the Grand River, a ¼ mile hike through the pasture owned by Jim Mason and his family, across the road from the Farm. He'd pack a lunch in a picnic basket and after swimming they would eat it on the shore next to the river or next to the waterfall on the twenty-foot cliff that overlooked the swimming hole. Usually nobody was swimming there, so it would be a private place for their date.

Harry had not been to this area for years; as a boy and teenager, he and Jim Mason and buddies had gone there to hang-out and swim. It had been fun then, and there was no reason why it would not be just as much fun, if not more fun, now with Ada.

As Harry was driving by the Mason farm, across the road from the Bradley farm, he saw Jim Mason, stripped to the waist and sweaty, mowing the lawn. He pulled his new Ford pick-up truck into the driveway and hailed Jim. Jim, with a wide smile on his face, hurried over to the truck and leaned both elbows on the window frame.

"Hi Jim, I've got a favor to ask. Would it be okay if I took my girlfriend through your place and back to the river to our old swimming hole?"

"Hey, old buddy, you didn't even need to ask, but thanks anyhow. Sure, go ahead anytime."

"Tomorrow afternoon, I think."

"How's your love life?" Jim asked. He always phrased his inquiry that way.

"I just know she's the woman I want to marry," Harry said confidently.""
"Been wondering when you would settle down, Harry"

"I'm glad Susie and I got married when we did". Susie was his high school sweetheart, and they married when he was 25 and she was 23. Now they had two toddlers who were presently in their sand box in the yard.

"Marriage seems to agree with you"

"It hasn't been all smooth sailing. We've had some petty arguments, but it's fun making up." We try never to go to bed angry."

Jim, thirty and he same age as Harry, was a tall well-built man, sandy haired, skin bronzed by the sun, and used to hard farm labor, the same as Harry. Harry caught himself fantasizing about the good sex that Jim and Susie must be having every night. Harry recalled how he and Jim swam naked in the river when they were teenagers and in their early 20s. He remembered how they became sexually aroused when they told each other about their abortive efforts with girls.

In his early twenties, Harry had dated an older divorced woman in Geneva, and he had spent many nights in her apartment. Their sex was good and he had asked her to marry him, but she had declined; she had met another man with more money and eventually married him.

Harry had another affair in his mid-twenties, and it had a similar course and ending. Harry did not want to strike out a third time, as he phrased it to himself. He would wait until the "right" woman came along.

He had been musing, but he remembered to ask, "How's Suzy?"

Jim had a wide smile on his face. He laughed. Then he said, "You know the old saying, 'Keep 'em barefoot in the winter and knocked up in the summer.'"

"You mean you're gonna hav e another kid?"

"Sure are."

"Congratulations!" Harry shook his friend's hand vigorously. "Well, I gotta be going" he said as he drove away.

Harry stopped at the Farm, asked Ada if she would like to go on a picnic and swimming with him that afternoon. "Be ready by 2:00 p.m.?"

"Yes, of course, it sounds like a lot of fun," she answered. She realized this was Harry's way of promoting himself and advertising, so to speak. It would give her a break, too, and a change of scenery. She wanted to hear more about skinny dipping. It sounded exciting Women should be allowed to skinny dip. Rick was nursing a wry smile. "It will probably result in an unwanted pregnancy, she was thinking. It was unfair. Men and boys had all the fun. Women and girls had to worry about pregnancy.

"American tradition, I think," said Harry.

"Why can't traditions be changed? said Ada.

"Yes, why not? said Harry.

This conversation took place sporadically while walking through the pasture. It helped to pass the time.

Harry had said, "Wear your bathing suit under your clothes. And wear long slacks. There may be poison ivy."

At 2:00 p.m. Harry arrived at the Farm wearing ragged blue jeans and a white sleeveless undershirt, and carrying a picnic basket and a blanket.

Then, off they walked to the pasture on the other side of the road. Harry set down the picnic basket and blanket and pulled up the barb wire so Ada could crawl beneath. Then, after standing on the other side, she reached down and held up the barb wire for Harry to crawl under.

Ada admired the muscular build of his naked arms. She could hardly wait to see him in swim trunks.

"Hope there are no bulls in this pasture," Ada said to make conversation as they walked along.

Harry smiled wryly. He said, "No. I'm the only one. My horoscope is Taurus, born in the month of May. What's yours?"

"Aries, born March 31ˢᵗ" she replied. This led her to a dead end. Sometimes it was hard to make small talk. Soon they were both sweating profusely. They saw five cows lying down in the shade of a hickory nut tree.

Harry said, "Those cows know when to take it easy. I'm soaked. Do you mind if I take off this undershirt?"

"No. of course not." She wished she could remove her blouse, but even though she was wearing her bathing suit beneath, she thought it would not be lady-like to take it off. She'd suffer it out.

"Whew, that feels better," he said as he tucked the wet shirt into his belt.

Ada had not seen his naked torso before, and she marveled at how handsome he was. With very little body hair and skin the color of bronze, he excited her. Just gazing at him was exciting and pleasurable.

It was the kind of late fall day Ada had dreamed about during the dark and dreary days when she was confined within the farmhouse. Today the clear blue sky was almost free of clouds. The leaves on many of the trees were still a vivid green.

It felt good to be alive on this beautiful day and on a swimming and picnic date with this handsome man who was very much in love with her. She knew she could learn to love him too. What about the Judge and his marriage proposal? She'd forget about him for now. She did not want to spoil her good time with Harry.

Harry knew the names of some plants and trees they walked by. He pointed out the abundance of crab apple trees of all sizes and wild flowers such as Queen Ann's Lace, Tiger Lilies, Daisies, and Goldenrod. Ada knew some of the names but not as many as Harry.

At last they came to the high bank of the Grand River. "I want you to see this waterfall," he said as led her by the hand to the cliff. Looking down, Ada saw the water in a shallow foot-wide stream suddenly plunge vertically downward and over a rock outcropping. "It's only about 20 feet high, but I've always thought of it as a miniature Niagara Falls." Harry said.

"When we were young guys, Jim Mason and I used to come skinny dipping here."

Ada was almost afraid to ask her next question. She wanted to hear more about skinny dipping. It sounded exciting, but it could result in unwanted pregnancy, it was unfair; the boys and men had all the fun, and the girls and women had to be worried about being pregnant.

"American tradition I think. It just feels great." Said Harry.

"Women should be allowed to do this," Ada said. It should be one of the fundamental rights for women., if they choose."

Rick was nursing a wry smile. Finally he said, "It will probably be many decades before women are given the same rights and privileges as men. End of lecture."

"Follow me" Harry said. "I'll show you the secret path down to the river." He led her along a trail that zig-zagged along the hillside. At last, after nearly losing her balance, she emerged at the water's edge. The beach had very little sand. It was mostly composed of gray well-weathered flat shale rocks. Harry set down the picnic basket and pulled down his blue jeans. When Ada saw him in his tight black trunks, she was momentarily breathless. *He's even more handsome and sexy-looking than I imagined, she said to herself.*

He laughed and showed the deep dimples in his cheeks. "Last one in is a rotten egg." He waded into the river. "Come on, Ada. The water's warm."

She stepped out of her slacks, unbuttoned her blouse and removed it. "Hey, you look great," Harry yelled. It was the first time she had worn the black one-piece bathing suit, and she was thankful it still fit.

She waded into the water and joined Harry in the chest-deep water.

"It doesn't get much deeper," Harry said. "It's an ideal swimming hole. Most of the water is too shallow to swim in. He said, "The water is about 85 degrees."

"Spread your legs," Harry said. He then dove under water and swam between her legs. Emerging, he shook the water out of his eyes and said, "We always used to do this. Sometimes you'd be swimming under four or five pairs of legs."

"I don't like to swim under water." Ada said. "It messes up my hair."

Suddenly Ada saw a long gray snake swimming about three feet from where they were standing. It frightened her so much she jerked backward quickly, lost her balance, and fell against Harry's chest. He wrapped his arms around her and kept her from going underwater. "Harry, did you see that snake? Why didn't you tell me there were snakes in here?"

"I saw it. They've never bothered us. They are more scared of us than we are of them. They always swim away when we are in here."

"It looked like it was three feet long."

"Some folks call them water moccasins, but I think they are some other types of water snakes. Water moccasins are in the deep south, not here."

Harry was still holding her, and she liked the feeling of his bare skin on her shoulders and neck. As she remained there, Harry kissed her lightly on her shoulders and neck. Then he turned her about and kissed her on the lips. It was a long kiss, and she wrapped her arms around his naked back. He whispered in her ear, "I really love you, Ada. I think I will always be able to make you happy." He spoke so earnestly that she was nearly moved to tears. Why couldn't she return his love? Thoughts about the life of a farmer's wife intruded. She might be happy when they were lovey-dovey and having sex, but what about all the rest of the time? Life on a farm could be stultifying. But also the quality of life in a small town could be the same. Ada recalled reading the novel Main Street, the satirical novel by Sinclair Lewis about a woman's life in a small town. Farm life could be undesirable, especially that of the wife of a poor chicken farmer.

She heard Harry whispering "I could make you very happy right now if you let me." It was the first time he had alluded to a sexual relationship.

She was not really insulted. She knew that young people were freer now than previously, that they were engaged in premarital sex. From what little Harry had told her, she assumed that he had slept with other women. She realized that he was trying desperately to make her fall in love with him.—that he would use his body, if necessary, to make this happen. All she needed to say was, YES or NO, and he would obey either command.

"I'd like to, Harry. I think I really would, but I can't. I want to wait until marriage.

"Okay," Harry said, sounding disappointed. They swam around the swimming hole for about fifteen minutes and then waded up to the rocky beach. Harry opened the picnic basket and removed everything, including a blanket he had thoughtfully placed in the bottom. He spread it on the rocks and they sat down, letting the sun's hot rays dry them off. They ate the ham sandwiches Harry brought and the potato salad Ada made that morning. Harry opened the thermos and poured out cups of cold cider they drank while eating the chocolate cake.

"Delicious," Ada commended. "Your mother knows how to bake." This sounded inane and superficial after Harry's offer of sex and her refusal.

After they finished eating, Harry packed everything except the blanket in the picnic basket. Then he said, "Let's lie down here for a while and just rest." When he was in a comfortable position, he turned his head toward her and said, "Why don't you want to marry me, Ada?"

"Harry, I'm still thinking about it."

"Has that Judge 'Appleby got you confused? I heard he's an old man. He cannot do for you what I can do for you. You know that."

"No, He's not that old. I'm 34 and he's in his early forties—about ten years older."

"He's a lot older than that—more like mid-fifties, even close to 60. Do you really want to marry an old geezer like that?"

"Harry, I don't want to hear you talking like that. He's really a very nice man, and he says he loves me."

"That's just a line he uses to get you to say YES.

"Harry, haven't you been using the same line to get me to say YES too? She knew she had him "by the balls," as she phrased it to herself. She was a lady, and she would never voice those cruel words.

CHAPTER 6

IN THE MEANTIME Judge Appleby had been stepping up the pressure on Ada to make a decision in his favor and he continued to do so during the months of November and December, 1930.

In early December he drove her in his snazzy 1930 chrome yellow Ford Victoria automobile to see a house in Salem on the Lake he was planning to buy if they married. They sat in his car and waited for the real estate agent to show up. Meanwhile they gazed at the house. It was a cold day, but it had not snowed. He kept the engine and heater running.

The house was located in a prestigious area of Salem on the Lake—The West End, as the townspeople called it. Its architecture—influenced by Frank Lloyd Wright—had some of the typical modern features. It was a sprawling red brick bungalow with a long front porch, its roof supported by brick columns. The second story had a long dormer in the front with four windows and a long sloping roof with windows in the rear.

The real estate agent, dressed in a multi-colored plaid overcoat, took them inside. The house was empty. The owner had already moved to California. The rooms were large and Ada visualized how they would look after redecorating. She disliked the wallpaper, but that could be removed and the walls papered or painted to her taste.

The first floor consisted of a living room with fireplace, dining room, kitchen, back porch, library, a maid's room with its own bathroom, and a separate half bath off the main hallway. Upstairs were three large bedrooms and two bathrooms,

Will said, "Ada, are these enough bathrooms to suit you?"

"Yes. At least I won't have to carry urinals to the outhouse."

"No more trudging through snow and ice. You will be marrying for the sole purpose of having clean bathrooms!"

"Not really for that sole purpose." She added.

"Thank God you are not marrying me for my money. I was beginning to have doubts."

Ada needed time to make the proper reply. "Please, Will, let's not talk about money. Okay?" "Let me see the basement." It was a walk-out basement. Unfinished, Ada thought it had definite possibilities. She visualized finishing the basement and having a playroom, recreation room, bathroom, and canning kitchen down there. Maybe even a couple of small bedrooms if needed. Being constructed on the crest of a hill composed largely of sand and gravel, the house had excellent drainage.

Ada realized it was one of the largest and most luxurious houses she had ever been in.

Judge Appleby asked the real estate man, "How big is this lot?"

"Pretty close to three acres." He led them to the rear of the house where they inspected the three-car garage, the patio, the garden area, the existing fruit trees—cherry, plum, German prune, apple, peach and pear—and two grape arbors.

Ada had asked Will about furniture. He said. "I have some." and then proceeded to list them—bookcases, desk, a couch, Morris chair, law books, the Century Encyclopedia, other books such as novels, et cetera. Before Ada could interrupt him, he said, "We'll go to Cleveland or Indianola and buy new furniture for the rest of the house."

Ada was flabbergasted. She did not know anybody who could furnish an entire house in one fell whoop. Anyhow she said, "How about the rest of your furniture?"

"It's not in very good condition. I'm planning to let it go with the Liberty Street house. I'll give the furniture to the people who buy the house.

"I'd like for you and me (or I as English language experts claim) to start our marriage with all new furniture that we have chosen together. No hang-overs from the past. Start with a clean slate."

This was good news for Ada, the one time he had taken her to his three-story Victorian house on Liberty Street, she had despised the dreary and shabby look of all his furniture—brown bulbous sofas and lounge chairs, Mission oak tables and chairs, heavy Mission oak bedroom sets, worn-out rugs.

Ada hated to admit being strongly lured by this new red brick house that Judge Appleby said he was prepared to buy. It was only two years old, having been built in 1928. _

Perhaps Papa was right, she reflected some days during the cold snowy winter months. Perhaps she could love this nice man who appeared to be so rich and generous.

Winters, because of the lake effect were severe in this northeastern corner of Ohio. Travel was hazardous on icy and snow-covered roads, so she did not have any more dates with the Judge.

But she often saw Harry; he would stop at the Farm after delivering eggs to customers in Geneva. Sitting side by side on the antique maple settee in the sitting room, they would cuddle and kiss when they were alone. Frequently Harry brought little gifts—boxes of candy, costume jewelry. Ada was moved by his earnestness and his absolute adoration of her. She finally said, after a torrid kissing session, "I really do love you, Harry."

On Monday, February 2nd, 1931, she went out to the mailbox and was surprised to see a letter from Judge Appleby. She took it up to her bedroom to read in private.

"Dear Ada :

I have missed you all winter. I am very lonely. The real estate agent has been pressuring me to make an offer on the house. He says another party has contacted him. If I do not make an offer soon, he will sell it to them. So I need to know your answer soon. "WILLYOU MARRY ME? Love, Will"

Without consulting her parents, she sat down at the little table in her upstairs bedroom and wrote:

"Dear Will:

I'm going to be perfectly honest with you. I am in love with Harry and he is in love with me. Though I can't quite picture myself as the wife of a chicken farmer, I know I have never loved a man like I love Harry. I appreciate the good times you've shown me and your wonderful offer of marriage, but I can't in all honesty marry you. Sincerely, Ada.

After sealing the envelope, she put on her boots, bundled up, and walked to the corner general store to mail it. She did not want their parents to know what she had done.

On Thursday, February 5th, 1931, she received another letter from the Judge:

"Dear Ada: I can't tell you how much anguish and sorrow I've experienced since reading your letter. I do love you Ada, and I can give you so much more than Harry can. I've decided that life without you is not worth living. My life and work are meaningless if I have to live alone, and you are the ONE I want to spend the rest of my life with. The future looks so bleak and empty that I might even contemplate taking my own life. Now I can fully understand why people commit suicide. I have a small pearl-handled revolver. It would be a fast and easy way for me to end it all. Please reconsider and marry me. All my love, Will"

This sudden turn of events astounded her. What should she do next? She had never received a letter like this in her life. The first idea she had was that he was faking it. *He wouldn't kill himself. That's just a ruse to get me to marry him. I wonder how many men have used this line.*

She did not show the letter to her parents, and the image of the Judge shooting himself remained with her all that day. *After she went to bed, it brought on a horrible nightmare: The scene was at the Farm. Two policemen knocked on the back kitchen door and demanded to see Ada. They told her that the Judge had shot himself and showed her a note found beside his body: If you want to know what happened, ask Ada Bradley Stevens—RD #2, Harpersfield, Ohio.*

She screamed when she read the note and woke up. Janet, sleeping beside her, also woke up and cried. She quickly pulled her daughter to her bosom, saying over and over

"There, there Mommy just had a bad dream." Finally the little girl ceased crying and fell asleep again. She was thankful that Rick, now nearly three years old and sleeping in his crib, did not wake up. Eventually Ada fell into a troubled sleep.

She awakened early while her children were still asleep and dressed. The plank floor was ice cold on her bare feet.' Her first chore was to empty the white chamber pot beneath the bed. Gingerly, she picked il up and carried it downstairs to the kitchen. She took her coat and hat from the pegs beside the door and bundled up. It was still snowing and windy.

She carried the chamber pot to the outhouse, removed the lid, and dumped its stinking contents into the hole. As she was doing this, she thought: *If I marry Harry I'll be doing this the rest of my life. His new house won't have indoor plumbing either and may never have it. If I marry the Judge I'll have indoor plumbing and three bathrooms. If I marry Harry I'll be forever bathing in the kitchen, using water boiled on the stove.*

She figured these were practical matters she ought to consider. Could her romantic love for Harry endure lifetime chores of carrying and emptying chamber pots filled with urine and feces? Then he pots had to be cleaned—disgusting and gross!

She hated having to tell Harry the bad news, but it had to be done. She could not remain with her parents forever; they had little money and her ex-husband Marion sent no money whatsoever.

So, on a day in early March when he stopped after his egg delivery, she told him. He laid his head on her shoulder and cried. She felt rotten about it, but it had to be done. She wrote a letter to the Judge, accepting his proposal of marriage, and she and the Judge were married by a Justice of the Peace in Jefferson, Ohio, on April 4th, 1931.

He took his new wife for a one-night, two-day honeymoon in Cook's Forest, Pennsylvania. He had to be back on the bench at the Salem on the Lake Municipal Court on Monday morning. The bride's mother Ada said to her husband Homer, "That's not enough time for two people (a man and a woman) to get to know each other."

"As I recall, Homer, it took you a long time."

"Let's not talk about it right now," Homer said. At the moment they were seated in the new wing chairs in the sitting room. They were relieved to know that Ada would have a nice home for herself and children. They knew, from their own experience, it was no fun living with in-laws. It felt so good to have a home of one's own.

For Ada it was a dream come true. She looked forward to the arrival of furniture trucks from Cleveland. It was fun moving heavy things around or watching her husband and grandsons do the heavy lifting. Ada and her friend Marie planned and sponsored a cookout for friends and neighbors

One afternoon later in the Fall Ada and Marie were lounging in the redecorated family room. One topic led to another and another and eventually to sex. Marie held up a newspaper advertisement and said, "Here's an ad for nude male dancers. Why don't we go?'

"Oh, Marie, Do you really want to go?"

"Sure. It will be fun. It's on Boys' night out. What does the rest of the ad say?"

"Two handsome fun-loving dudes will do it all for you—a slow strip-tease all the way down. Afterwards make a date with one or more of us. Free consultation"

"Doesn't it sound wonderful?" Marie exclaimed

Ada was more skeptical.

"Well, Will, You know our problem, don't you?" Ada said. It seems we discussed it before. Refresh my memory.'

"You said the Judge was impotent."

"Oh, yes, now I remember. Right after we got married and we were trying to get me pregnant, it must have worked. I'm pregnant now for Martin.

I'm due in December.

"So you're in the market for some fresh meat," Marie said.

"You make it sound too forbidden."

"You're bored silly and so am I. Let's get ready. Wednesday, wear your most outlandish and seductive gown. Make sure you wear a long winter coat over the gown, and bring plenty of one dollar bills to stick into their skimpy jockstraps."

And so, they met the two young men who did all the things they said they would.

The young men lived in a restored Victorian house with four bedrooms and two bath rooms. The men were fond of photos and pictures of naked people—men and women in compromising positions. Ada and Eva thought it was exciting to see, on the wall or ceiling what they were doing on the bed.

The two women felt no guilt for their actions. The Judge may have been suspicious, but he did not investigate. The men did not feel any guilt. It was the ideal situation for all parties involved.

CHAPTER 7

ADA AND EVA never told their respective husbands about their deception. At family gatherings they were very discreet. Eventually they tired of this cat and mouse game and told their male lovers goodbye.

C.W. or Will as he preferred to be called was grateful for Ada's help as he grew older. He continued to be re-elected as the years sped by. He tolerated Rick's chicken business in the old double garage. Throughout Rick's teenage years he had saved money in his own bank account in Citizens Savings and Loan. He did not boast about it, but in his senior year in high school he figured he'd saved enough. He needed a decent-looking coat for school, so he went to Whitneys, and picked out a green corduroy jacket with a warm lining. He picked out some matching pants and a green felt hat with a single white feather.

It was now the middle of April, and he was beginning to think about his education. Because of the money he spent on clothing, he would need more money.

One day Rick said to his mother, "It seems that the more money you get, the more you suddenly need." When the Judge saw Rick's new clothes, he laughed and made fun of them. He said, "That white feather is just the ticket. HA HA."

Aunt Fanny came to his high school graduation dinner and told about the GI BILL and the money supplied by the Federal Government. $75 per month would be available for living expenses and more would be available for tuition and books. For Rick, this was a dream coming true. "Isn't that great?" Aunt Fanny said."

The Judge slapped the palms of his hands together and said, "That is the worst thing that could happen. We are on the road to Socialism and Communism, and there is no turning back. You mark my words The Federal Government is already taking a big hunk of your money. Pretty soon they'll have a lot more."

Rick exclaimed, "I'm going to sign up for the U.S. Amy tomorrow morning. The recruiting officer has been after me. Rick was true to his word. He enlisted for three years.

CHAPTER 8

ADA WAS PLEASED that Rick was going into the Army and eventually to college but she knew she would miss him terribly. She kept a stiff upper lip as she embraced him for the last time before boarding the brown Army bus. It's funny she said to herself, "Eighteen years ago, I was embracing a little toddler before he boarded the big yellow school bus. I cried then as I am crying now. Time goes so fast I can't keep track of it. He is such a nice young man. I feel he may be too conscientious and volunteer for some dangerous task."

"Rick," she said. "Do write me a letter now and then."

"Yes Mom. I will." He climbed the steps and was at a window" waving goodbye, Mom."

Again, Rick was true to his word. He wrote his first letter home on July 22, 1946. "Just got word this morning that we are shipping out today at 9:00 a.m. we have to turn in or bedding. They have not told us exactly where we are going but it will be either Texas or Alabama. Don't send any of my things yet until I send you the address of our new camp. We get up every morning at 5am. We have to have our lights out at 11p.m. Any time we go anywhere we have to wait in lines. Some are blocks long. This camp (Atterbury) is just like a big city. There are streets, stores and PX stores (Post Exchange Stores). There you can buy anything at a reduced price. You can go to a movie for 15 cents and you get into the service club free."

"There are kids here from all over the country. Most of them are sent to basic training camps within a week or two.

"We took I.Q. tests yesterday. I didn't do very well in mine. Also, we took a radio test, but I didn't even pass that. The day before yesterday we got our clothes, uniforms, and a dozen other things."

"Then on June 24, 1946 we heard we were shipping out tonight, I mean tomorrow morning. I am going to Fort Sam Houston, Texas. Most of my buddies are going to Fort Knox, Kentucky. I just hope that the camp in Texas won't be too hot. It will take about two days and two nights to get there. I'll send my new address when I get there. Today I had detail office work. I worked at the insurance office."

Like the children of war-torn London, Rick and fellow soldiers never knew where they were going until the train got them there. Rick wrote, "We came to Camp Lee, Virginia, instead of going to Texas."

While Rick was having basic training and rifle training and endless marching, the Judge was inwardly rejoicing that he did not have Rick "under foot." He enjoyed the freedom to pursue his own interests. He could pick up a murder mystery novel and keep reading until he finished the entire book. Often he would boast to Ada and Vi about his reading speed. He would also claim to be able to; write a better novel.

"Then why don't you?' Ada would angrily reply.

"My dear young lady, you have no conception of the work involved—the research. I'd be spending all my spare time at the Library."

"Well, you like to read"

Later, Ada reiterated: "You are not the home handyman, and you don't lift your hand or arm to do the things most husbands do willingly.'

The Judge said, "You married me for better or for worse."

What the Judge kept to himself was his collection of erotic and pornographic literature. He resolved to try out some of the so-called modern techniques. He'd try one of them tonight.

Thinking about it gave his flabby penis an almost instant hard-on. There was still hope for an old man.

CHAPTER 9

AS THE YEARS sped by, the Judge enjoyed his new freedom or escape from Rick. While Rick was growing up he claimed his mother's full attention, especially after being bawled out by the Judge over a simple infraction of the household rules.

This one was Rule #2—"If you turn it on, turn it off." The Judge insisted that all the lights be turned off at 10 p.m. On special occasions, the time could be advanced to 10:30 p.m.

The Judge found a plaque containing the 12 rules of Basic Training In a gift shop while touring the Smokey Mountains. He made copies. Back home he hung one copy in each room of the house.

One evening he had all family members gather in the Library. "He gave a copy to each person including himself. "Follow along as I read them to you"

Ada was extremely angry. She raised her voice. "You are treating us like idiots. We can read." She repeated. "We can Read." "This is an insult to our intelligence."

"No Way. These are rules that can be easily followed and will simplify our lives. Rick is all the time writing letters and telling of all the Army rules he has to follow."

Ada spoke sharply, "I didn't think you read any of Rick's letters—that you thought they were silly and immature. So, have you changed you mind? You've always treated Rick and me as far below your level of intelligence, that we were intellectually inferior to you —our great Lord and Master. You've always talked down to me and Rick."

"Then, why on earth didn't you ask for a divorce?"

And let you use lawyer tricks to leave me high and dry without an adequate income. You have spoiled me. I can't settle down to a rocking chair existence and you know it"

"This kind of talk in front of Vi and the hired men is getting us nowhere. (They were in the Library.) I move we adjourn. In the meantime, read and study those rules."

Ada said, "Amen, and goodnight."

Vi, who had stayed with the Applebys and Bradleys over the years, said, "We need to show more love and understanding." She was almost like a second mother to Rick (myself) and Martin. With the help of a lady friend, she had taken up the study of Christian Science.

That night As Ada and the Judge were undressing for bed, the Judge said, "Well, Ada, what do you think of those twelve rules?"

"They are all just common sense, common horse sense. I don't need them. Rick doesn't need them."

"But most people who do stupid things would benefit. They should follow DDDT —Don't do dumb things."

"You like to make up catchy slogans."

"Yes, I do —if they help to make our lives simpler and safer.'"

The Judge, naked as the day he was born, slipped under the covers while his wife was in the bathroom.

Upon entering the cocoon of sheets and blankets, Ada exclaimed, "Wonder of wonders will never cease. You have a gigantic hard-on that needs immediate treatment. She threw back the covers and stripped out of her nightgown, and seemingly pounced upon the naked Judge. She said, "Now, tell me, Judge, "Which one of those twelve rules is most appropriate?"

"Actually all of them are," the old Judge said, maybe #5 and #7. A list of the 12 rules is printed below:

1. If you open it, close it.
2. If you turn it on, turn it off.

3. If you unlock it, lock it.
4. If you break it, repair it.
5. If you can't fix it, call in someone who can.
6. If you borrow it, return it.
7. If you use it, take care of it.
8. If you make a mess, clean it up.
9. If you move it, put it back.
10. If it belongs to someone else, get permission to use it.
11. If you don't know how to operate it, leave it alone.
12. If it does not concern you, don't mess with it.

CHAPTER 10

ADA HAD TO admit to herself that the old Judge was a good fornicator. She smiled when she realized she might follow Rule #5 in case the Judge could not perform sexually. Rule #5 stated "If you can't fix it, call in someone who can." Does that rule also apply to sexual problems? A clever lawyer could probably make it apply. Because of her husband's success as a practicing attorney, she had the belief that clever lawyers could work miracles.

Another evening Ada and the Judge were alone in their house. Martin and Rick were out with their friends. The old Judge was feeling horny, wondering what kind of sexual mischief the boys might get into. He climbed into bed and said to Ada, "How about letting me show you something that is anything but boring?"

"I was wondering when you were going to show me one of your sexy tapes. I hope that Martin and Rick have not beaten you to it."

"They probably have seen everything labeled PORN-" The Judge had stored tapes, discs, magazines and books in a cardboard box on the top shelf of their master bed room. Ada was very interested. This was was one of her first voyages into the world of pornography. While watching some xxx rated acts, she snuggled up to the Judge's naked back. He had thoughtfully removed his clothes so he could be stark naked. She slid out of her nightgown. She whispered into his ear, "Can we do these things?. They are wild. I can't wait until I get your body ln the right position."

"Sweetie, if you talk like that, you'll make me come too soon."

"I want to see you come. I've heard that some guys can come many times. Can you?"

"No, sweetie, I'll be doing good if I can come once or twice. That night he managed to come twice. While his wife was in the bath room he looked in the box again. To his displeasure he observed that a couple of discs were missing; He must have overlooked them in his rush to have sex. He told himself he should find a better hiding place—perhaps a hollowed-out center in an outdated law book. A hiding place was a temporary solution. A more permanent one would be the safe in the basement of their brick bungalow; the problem was that he had misplaced the combination.

"Oh well" he sighed, "I can hollow out some outdated law books and let the future generations of Applebys and Bradleys have the fun of discovering them."

Early the next morning the Judge was awakened by his lusty wife. The Judge was wearing only a Jockey brief. Ada, wearing only a transparent garment, quickly tore it away from her hips and whispered, "Darling, I want to undress you and worship your naked flesh."

He said, "Where did you get this vocabulary?"

Ada said, "I look at the same magazines you do." She hesitated to say more. "Did you look at Play Girl's Calendar?" Ada grasped both legs of his briefs and pulled them down. Released suddenly from its tight habitat, the eight inch hard-on sprang into action and vibrated back and forth several times.

The Judge regarded these experiences as proof that he had feet of clay, that he was a normal human male. He might be able to satisfy Ada's sexual needs. He knew for sure Ada and Eva were visiting at least two virile and handsome men who were living in a restored Victorian house. Because of his good relationship with the police department, he was able to have his wife Ada tracked.

He would not reveal any of his discoveries to Ada until some future time. He told himself it may never happen.

The detective showed the Judge several photographs of Ada and Eva, both stark naked, making links in a human chain.

The Judge started to vomit. He went behind a shrub to finish. Luckily they were seated on a park bench in one of the town's parks. Nobody else was around.

The Judge was in need of a glass of a glass of water. After getting into the detective's car, the detective said "Duck down in the back seat." The detective drove to the nearest fast food restaurant. He gave a glass of water to the Judge who vomited then gargled. That was enough excitement for one day.

CHAPTER 11

THE TIME WAS in the latter part of June, 1946, and Rick Stevens had just joined the United States Army, Quartermaster Corps. The recruiting officer said that a big brown-painted school bus (formerly yellow) would be taking a bus-load of young men like himself to Cleveland for a two-day physical and mental examination. The local recruiting officer did not know when the bus would arrive at Salem on the Lake. But, be ready! He told Rick to fill a small gym bag with personal items—tooth brush, tooth paste. Shaving cream and razor Two pairs of underpants, T-shirts, and a couple of pocket books to read and pass the time when waiting for some officer to examine him.

CHAPTER 11

"Now is the time for all good men to come to the aid of their country."

Rick Stevens idly typed this sentence on special paper for his journal. Later, computer users would call it hard copy.

World War II had ended. The Korean had not yet started. The Korean years of peace were what Rick and thousands of young men like him looked forward to. The time was now in the month of June, of 1946. Rick had just joined this peace -time Army and was looking forward to his next year at the University of Virginia and also renewing his romance with Catherine Hudson.

He gave scant attention to what he would be studying. When asked, he said he was enrolled in a Pre-Medical Program.

"So you want to be a doctor?" his half bother Martin teased.

Rick defended himself, saying "Just shut up. It's none of your business."

When Catherine asked the same question, he replied, "In my home town of Salem on the Lake, the doctors are the richest men in town. Their families are the richest."

Rick's step-father the Judge took a sudden interest in Rick after he received a letter from Rick, requesting some career information. This was the era when career guidance was virtually unknown. The Judge was flattered to be asked. He did a lot of thinking and then answered with a one sheet, single-spaced thoughtful and kind letter, transcribed below:

'THE MUNICIPAL COURT
Salem on the Lake, Ohio

Dear Rick

I was glad to receive your letter this morning. There must always be a first time, you know as I remember, I have written you but once or twice, but we should have corresponded more frequently'.

Now, about your college course: I am happy that you have the ambition to study for a profession, but have you carefully looked ahead with the long thought? Do you think naturally that you would be equipped for the practice of medicine and surgery? Do you have a natural leaning or compulsion along this line and a strong liking for that kind of work?

You must remember that the medical course is one of the very hardest. There will be four years of college for a Bachelor's degree and then four years more in medical college and afterwards one or two years as an intern at which time you will be about 31 years of age.

The government will provide, in large part, for your college courses, but what about the next four years? I feel certain considering the amount of hard study needed and necessary to complete the medical course that you would not be able to work your way through.

I know it is easy for a young man to say, "I would like to be a doctor or a lawyer, but he needs to consider most carefully and earnestly, whether he has a real and natural bent along the course to be pursued, and whether he feels reasonably certain that he can make a success for his life work, and whether he is particularly suited for it.

After all, you must decide for yourself, but have you considered a business administration course, or some similar course? You would save four to six years and get in some lucrative position when you are about 25 or 26. Of course, a university offers a multiplicity of courses, some of which fit the peculiar talents and natural tendencies of every student."

Rick found a quiet corner where he could study this carefully composed letter. He had made arrangements with two college friends from Ohio State, and with Chuckie Olmstead, Rick's boyhood companion in his home town. They had been talking about and planning this Western Trip for several months. At the moment they had maps spread out on the dining room table. Each of the men had saved several hundred dollars and planned to find reasonably priced motel rooms. They would rent rooms with two double beds. At home they all slept in single beds. To save money for the trip, they would have to get used to sharing a bed. It was a small sacrifice to make for seeing those gigantic mountains and other sights. It was a Sunday and they were packed and ready to take off. Their parents dutifully walked out to the car and saw them off. The Judge recalled some of his early adventures. The last thing he said was, "Don't do anything I would not do"

The last thing that Ada whispered in Rick's ear as she hugged him was "Keep it in your pants."

The Judge added a personal note to his letter. Rick, in his haste, had forgotten this paragraph. "Your mother and I will probably drive to the Finger Lakes Region in New York State, visiting Cornell, for our vacation. You and your friends will have a most memorable trip to the West, one you will never forget. Love, Dad"

For the last few years the Judge had been-- not loving, not exactly friendly either. He treated Rick more like an employee who was reliable. He had asked Rick to type his letters—both business and personal. There were many letters to Martin. He praised his son for the excellent grades he was earning.

The Judge, over time, made changes in his behavior. Rick told his mother that the Judge was actually treating Rick with respect. Ada said, "I think he is mellowing with age. He seems to have given up his pretense of being innately superior to most men ".

Rick read his stepfather's letter, recommending that he major in business administration several times. He told himself and his mother, in a letter. It was sage advice, but he did not tell this to the Judge. The phrase "sage advice." sounded too intimidating, disrespectful to the Judge.

Rick clung to the false belief that he could somehow master all the myriad details of a medical and scientific education. For three years he plodded along. Finally it was in an organic chemistry course that the dam broke. The professor had been busy making chalk diagrams on the blackboard. He had chalk in his right hand and an eraser in his left hand. He was speaking in a half whisper. The stock joke among the students who were hanging onto every word was, "Turn up your hearing aids."

Rick decided to break the news to his three close friends—Chuckie Olmstead, Perry Longacre and AJ Stockman. They were Pre-Medical students who had not given up. They were smart, motivated, and had well-do-do parents willing and able to invest more funds for the education of their sons.

Chuckie's parents ran a profitable sand and gravel business, selling and delivering many truckloads to concrete road builders. Perry's father was Dr. Longacre who had a profitable business as a family doctor. Al Stockman's parents were teachers at the local high school.

Finally after goodbyes were exchanged and cautions against speeding were given for the tenth time, Chuckie backed his new burgundy convertible Buick out of the driveway

While climbing the front steps, and the stairs to the master bedroom, Ada said, "It feels so good to be free to take off and to have the house empty for a while. Let's open that bottle of champagne, then watch one of your sexy movies."

The Judge said, "Sounds like a good game plan to me, but you know how unpredictable I am."

"I'LL TAKE A CHANCE," Ada said. With that, she stood up and began stripping. She swung each item like she'd seen those naked guys do it in her husband's sexy movies.

The Judge began removing his clothes, carefully folding them. When she came to her underpants she stopped to tease. Then her husband began his own kind of strip tease. Ada wondered just how the Judge knew about their clandestine activities.

A few days later the lady doctor at the Clinic telephoned and set up an appointment for C.W.

The lady doctor who examined him rather thoroughly said, "It is too bad he surrendered his good body to tobacco and alcohol."

"Don't tell me to stop smoking or drinking. It didn't work before."

"If you keep on doing now what you have been doing this past year, you will be lucky to live more than a year." The lady doctor spoke slowly and emphatically. She said, "X-rays don't lie. Get your affairs in order."

The Judge knew the end was coming soon.

For wont of human companionship the Judge began to see a lot of movies. He took his family when he could talk them into going with him. One memorable film was LUTHER. He and Ada enjoyed seeing it together. One time he stopped at the town library and looked up information in the Encyclopedia Britannica. It was heavy reading for an elderly man who had vague memories of hearing about Martin Luther (1483-1546) in college lectures.

He often said, "It's too bad that a man cannot live long enough to read all the important books. I am attempting this task and am re-reading books I read in school and college."

Rick was now living at home and helping with the Judge's letters, using an Underwood typewriter. He also composed some letters. As the Judge grew older, his handwriting deteriorated.

Rick was engaged with teaching the sciences—chemistry and general sciences one year and physics and general sciences the following year. The first two years Rick also had to teach biology. His evenings at home and weekends and vacation days were crammed with work—his own and that of the Judge This work lasted eight years, until the consolidation of high schools in the county. Since Rick preferred teaching older students, he was out of a job.

Through a family friend, he was able to teach in a suburban Cleveland high School. This job lasted only one year. Rick misread the contract. It was for only one year. Next, Rick put an advertisement in the Cleveland Plain Dealer and in several other newspapers. He was really surprised by the number of responses. This time, he got what he asked for, a science teacher for PSSC physics in high schools. Rick had been a candidate for special training in several different summer sessions – Boston College, Fordham, and The University of Redlands, California. Residents of Salem on the Lake may recall, if they have saved newspaper clippings that the Judge of the local Municipal Court maintained his position up until a few days before his death. The Clerk of Court Ann Grant was able to keep the office running and give information to the judges until the next election. For seven days the Judge was an invalid in a hospital bed with many gadgets attached and an oxygen tent. As he grew weaker, he needed help with ordinary walking; he could not control his legs and needed help when going to the bathroom. The final two days the Judge wanted to return to his bed at 120 West Main Road, the long red brick ranch-style house in the West End of Salem on the lake. Many friends visited. They all reported that the Judge was rational until the very end of his life. He demonstrated he was a clear thinker. Rick can testify that these are true statements. Rick was with the Judge until the very end. His last words to Rick were "I love you." The nurses on duty also heard his words.

Local newspapers printed articles about his career. One of the best ones, *in* the eyes of the editors of the local newspapers was the following:

A SADDENED COMMUNITY MOURNS THE DEATH of Judge C. W. Appleby.

For 27 years the jurist bore the title, "Your Honor" with dignity and pride. His actions in office won him the widespread respect of the community.

Judge Appleby's life could easily form the basis of a motion picture— the entertainment he loved so well.

His grandfather pioneered this territory, pushed Great Lakes commerce, and took a daring active part in the abolitionist movement.

The Judge was a pioneer in his own right, for the first generation of settlers must always be followed by the generation which brings the safeguards of liberty to the land.

The mark of brilliance was on Judge Appleby when he passed the Ohio bar examination in 1898 with high marks, the second highest in the state. He fulfilled this promise when he became the first and only Judge of Municipal Court.

Judge Appleby pioneered the establishment of justice on a local level. From the bench, he balanced the scales of justice with neither unemotional harshness nor undue sympathy.

His fairness was known to defendant and prosecutor alike. The success of his long career was apparent in his record—only one reversal ln 27 years ON THE BENCH. He served conscientiously, with a keen mind, nearly to the very day of his death. Despite failing health and advancing years, Judge Appleby's death marks the end of an era on the Salem on the Lake scene.

It brings only sadness to the cop on his beat, the busy lawyer and the citizen in the street who was assured justice would prevail with Judge Appleby on the bench.

After Rick read this final sentence in the funeral home, he was saddened still further, thinking to himself; What is the value of a human life? Could the Judge improve his own life if he could live it over again? What about the Judge's extra-marital affairs with women in his own class? What about the judge's addiction to pornography? Do all these internal problems lessen his judgments as a human being? Whatever external problems existed, the Judge took care of them. He was a careful, neat and clean dresser. He was always pleasing for the town's eyes. He was careful not to offend minorities and individuals. He was a good provider for his family—always keeping them well supplied with groceries. He was a good story teller and teller of jokes. It's true he was addicted to alcohol and tobacco—chain smoking up to 100 cigarettes per day and drinking one glass of booze after another usually beer. Rick, the Judge's step-son lived with his step family the first 29 years of his life. In addition to teaching physics and earth science in the local high school, he typed letters and took care of the correspondence for the Judge.

Every day of my life I (disguised as Rick) have regretted not following a business education and work. The Judge said, in essence, that I (Rick) was cut-out for that kind of work. That was his sage advice which I should have followed. Still, Rick found himself haunted by the words of an ancient novelist—Bulwer Lyten: "The saddest words of tongue or pen are these few words: It might have been."

Later in life Rick pondered the words of his stepfather: "You are not cut out for the life of a Doctor of Medicine." "That is it. No ifs, ands, or buts." This was the final naked truth that Rick had to live with, but it seemed so arbitrary, so man-made, so unreal; yet it was the God awful truth.

He would have to adjust and prepare himself for a commercial education, as he had already begun while working for the Judge.

On the plus side, Rick had inherited a fine library with a variety of books dealing with many subjects, including medical ones such as anatomy and physiology. He shared many of them with his half-brother, Martin (Calvin Appleby) As of this writing, one year after the funeral of the JUDGE, the Applebys are still going strong in their three-story

64

mansion. They always invite me to their parties, and I usually attend. I've met and courted my future wife and will be attending one of the Appleby parties where I shall announce our future engagement.

I believe that the Judge would be happy knowing that the internal and external problems of families can be solved, that parties must be willing to compromise, that "Forgive and Forget" are not just idle words but are a vital part of the basic Christian philosophy. Also, this world is full of Good and Evil ideas and influences. Each person, at the appropriate times, must choose the right ones to follow. Rules for convenience and daily living are not the same as rules governing a basic philosophy or religion.

After all is said and done, more is usually said; Many people have said this besides myself. I'll stop now.

Love and Peace to all the people in the world.

FORGIVE AND FORGET

Printed in the United States
By Bookmasters